Stigmata

Stigmata

POEMS

SCOTT JACKSHAW

TALONBOOKS

Talonbooks
9259 Shaughnessy Street, Vancouver, British Columbia, Canada V6P 6R4
talonbooks.com

Talonbooks is located on xʷməθkʷəy̓əm, Sḵwx̱wú7mesh, and səlilwətaɬ Lands.

First printing: 2025

Typeset in Minion 3 and TC Antiquated
Printed and bound in Canada on 100% post-consumer recycled paper

Talonbooks acknowledges the financial support of the Canada Council for the Arts, the Government of Canada through the Canada Book Fund, and the Province of British Columbia through the British Columbia Arts Council and the Book Publishing Tax Credit.

Library and Archives Canada Cataloguing in Publication

Title: Stigmata : poems / Scott Jackshaw..
Names: Jackshaw, Scott, author.
Identifiers: Canadiana 20250184303 | ISBN 9781772016918 (softcover)
Subjects: LCGFT: Poetry.
Classification: LCC PS8619.A2355 S75 2025 | DDC C811/.6—dc23

for Britt and Mack

From now on, a wound is only a wound –
and the whole body's only a wound.

—JEAN-LUC NANCY

Corpus, translated by Richard A. Rand (2008)

Confession is, therefore, the closest
image we may have of hell.

—MARCELLA ALTHAUS-REID

The Queer God (2003)

Contents

Fig. 1 – 00:04

The Mystical Theology

What are the affirmative theologies and what are the negative?

I made a list of bright red holes.

I remembered a few names, a solid oak pulpit, or was it veneered.

I heard the many-voiced man. I saw the many lights. I called on fragile abstractions.

This was a body. That was a screen. There was never any doubt.

The supreme cause of perceptible things is not itself perceptible.

On Friday I bore the holes in my body.

I was not moving or at rest. I was not speaking, only next to speech. I needed to know – what is the divine gloom?

The holes often seeped blood, staining my tunic and briefs. Yes, my palms were swollen. Yes, my soles were stamped.

My mouth was the colour of a sun-dried tomato. The tomato was drawn from the world of sense and applied to the nature of god.

My nostrils were secondary. There was something more important at stake.

The supreme cause of conceptual things is not itself conceptual.

Those who bore the holes in their bodies were most often women or having borne them became women.

The name was vast and minuscule, wide and restricted, eloquent and concise.

I recalled the homosexual formula: I am my mother, my mother is me.

My lips were a prosthesis for feeling. For all feeling that was not feeling.

I found it hard to keep the holes clean and wondered if the holy women also struggled to wash their hands.

The supreme cause of conscious things is not itself conscious.

There was a baptist church on the south side of the city. Its congregants had never seen a bright red hole.

Did I look to strange hymnals? Did I love the mouth?

I proceeded openly and truthfully with my confessor.

The goal was to leave behind everything perceived and understood.

I took long walks on campus, caught up in the things of this world. I held to the exhaustion of encounter. I submitted to antibacterial soap.

The mysteries were simple and unyielding.

I knew that the fear of speech was close but not identical to the fear of god.

For a moment you'd broken through. I held you at the foot of the toilet bowl.

The supreme cause of red is not itself red.

I learned over lunch the forms of desire. I listened as they made a scar of sense. I didn't know what to want.

It seemed there were many rivers in my head and their waters hurtled downward not to my ears but to the part where they say the soul lives.

Who puked at the heels of angels. Who took meticulous notes. Who clenched and looked away.

I tried to drown a pastor in each poem. I couldn't leave them behind. The problem was formal anyway.

The problem was petechiae. There was no unpoliced surface. My mouth was a rash with five points.

This is why I don't like the word *mystical.*

I am so fearful as I write this that I don't know how I'm writing it or how I live when I think about it, which is very often.

The supreme cause of holes is not itself a hole.

When you rubbed my chest your hand slipped as often happens and touched a bright red hole. I felt great pain, pushed the hand away, and begged god to spare you.

Who is like the church? Who can make love to it?

I spat up air or stone. In this sprouting I was inexistent, lifeless, speechless, mindless.

By Saturday there remained only two means of entering and leaving the mouth. One was emissive, the other emetic.

I experienced such great noise in my head that I found it a hardship even to write.

The supreme cause of sexed things is not itself sexed.

The pronoun was a bright red hole. It wasn't a body. It didn't flower. It suffered no decay. It could be neither seen nor touched.

In other words it was more debt than meat. The accountants all died but the ledger remained.

There was little room for interpretation. All the same I refused to believe in mercy or inflation.

I prayed to a red god. I couldn't help it. I tore the spine of my notebook and passed my stones to the bowl.

If only concepts had real names.

The supreme cause of thinking things is not itself thinking.

I made bright red holes in my tongue, recalling the weight of you in my mouth. The speech pathologist was livid.

On Sunday I woke from the dream with a pressing need to micturate.

Here I hazard a border.

This was my body.

Say it again.

This was my body.

For how many? For how long? The more I climb the more language falters.

Bataille worried he'd written a book for everyone that would interest no one.

I was led away by bright red holes. It's a symptom of oral fixation.

The supreme cause of figurative things is not itself a figure.

Without a careful system of measurement there would be no faith or disappointment.

Those holes were the centres of the soul.

They were not number or sequence, greatness or smallness, ebb or flow. They were not here at least not in any sense I understand.

Nothing was more illegible. Nothing more perilous or common.

I wouldn't be surprised if god gave me this headache.

About three days have passed since I began. I'm in no condition to read over what I've written. Everything will have to continue without order.

Someday the holes will speak for themselves.

I don't meet god but contemplate its dwelling place.

I

Noise II

here is a ruined sound
my sonogram
swells with blood
gestates parliament
my sonant gut sprawls with racket
pulses and maps
yolk out talk
estrangement my
small weeks pass

Benediction

I surrendered to sweat every form that was abhorrent to me
fever stains on my mattress the yellow in my towels the rusted

shirts I couldn't bear I embellished their volumes their
surfaces who could say whether they'd become

an atmosphere an edema a flooded
street none of this could be verified

and there arose a great sewage in my body from which no
leak could save me I prayed to my melting god:

dissolve this architecture of relation and restore
vulgar feeling to everywhere hygiene has sterilized it

I was such a wide city with such wide sewers
there were no chunks no suspended things

the blood in my stool indexed a great unrest afloat in the
toilet's umber a great fear of drowning a great fear of touch

following the curvature of my gut the swerve
of my tubular passage I had turned shitless

as a bruise a pressing sore

gone loose in the runoff I built great
rubble to honour its impermanence it resembled fountains

Lapse

when you took my bed completely
when you became the pillow
when you printed your skin on the carpet
when I found quiet rhythms in my room
when I mistook you for the window shade
which could have been the chorus

haven't thrown away your sock
from under my bed what
does anyone resemble

Jubilee, 1978

the phosphorous entrail

I make my desiring pirouette by fire, history's ashen
decompression, the guts of capital dug out my chest

I have my piss on the cellophane fresh licked
television screens I have my nylon sense making

my trampled couture I'm wearing cinders

Noise III

here is a ruined sound
my blessed emulsion
being an emergency that precedes
categorical rib work
when I am taken up
to my wounding ground
the suicidal solvent
in subject time

Kenosis

In the undulation I induce thick broths on his cock. A state of material crisis conditions any worlding gesture.

Taxonomies of fucking emerge. Deep-time anality, slow exenteration, memorial touch, reflexive dislocations that accrue gut plastics, a crooked sternum, archaeoacoustics, its mouth where all difference is abolished, a cavernous ingrowth.

In the shower he thins puke down his popliteal rut. He is the blow job's long retch. An uttering fluid.

The pronoun falters. I soak him up.

I spill on desertion which is a pool where he pools on everything. On slipping he coats my scalp in so lonely clumps.

The traffic in barf reveals a terrible thing. History has no obligation to repeat itself. I'm holy with him in the toilet.

We spit up being in the act a breach that is god's name we feel it dizzy and know that all text exteriorizes the organ all residue marks the passing world.

Contrition

I scatter polities with my strange toe
a latent mystic sits on my thighs
home is a technology of baptism
god has become everything or nothing

I withhold myself
where is the portal to desire
his abyss face lingers or not
I leave thinly and draped in blankets

Some Theories of Atonement

In the planetary scar tissue where I follow you in our last
days together, where we sacrifice the clots of lawn, where
we do not become god but take on its bodies, in our body,
where we expose ourselves, in our body, which like our sex is
secret to us, in the plenary of flip-fucking, an experiment in
reading, in our therapy for root rot, the scriptures where you
learn to abuse, in our body, where we index the earth's pores,
in our body, which is consumption.

Here is touching a garden of crushed violet. Here is its stain.
Here is another pound of petals. Here is a name for culture.
Here is its culturing tongue.

I want to be wire, a tendon, a fig branch, an artery, a catalogue of reticulate forms, an orgy, a fibre. I want my solidarity with you exhausted. There you fashion a catalyst for rot. There you breathe me out. There you love and break the soil.

Into which we folded our failures of imagination: the
catachresis, the ligament, the vine, to crawl out on the blood,
help my unbelief in the body, a listening post at its borders,
the shape of its unremarkable terror, holding you, accidents
without substance, the copula between god and love, how
it felt to hold you, the bread, the winter jacket you left here,
the wine.

Noise IV

here is a ruined sound
my pulmonary shunt
bulbous hymn head
I engulf whole foyers
my radiant lung
unconjugated for
the soft pulpit nation

Intinction

a long way scattered so baked into earth you will be
the long remains you will gather iodine in thick lumps
you will strike rock it will serve as a mouth for you

over and over you will finish in a mouth for you

there will be weather: heavy with beds, heavy
with antihistamines, heavy sacks all day around
the garden, long with dew, heavy leaden waves

you will have planted all of it you will fall
where the flower bed marks your thickest breath

what follows has been a layer of dust that once
every second glossed the surface of dead time

in hand this rod with which you perform

before a funeral is a funeral lingering

Reparation

something must be put into phrases

leans into my distant splinter, a door
prolapses, I spoil my crust with dirt

with the water stains on my ceiling, lamp full of moths
bending floor of my desire

I summer with myself, palms
drain, as he speaks my side
spills over the picnic table

choke down mushrooms with my
ex-boyfriend and ex-girlfriend, nailheads rise
from my palms, a shower head opens, the long bed watches
I am a city of knees

Stalker, 1979

the thought is in me again

a flood tunnel empties

belief is the grammar of mutilation

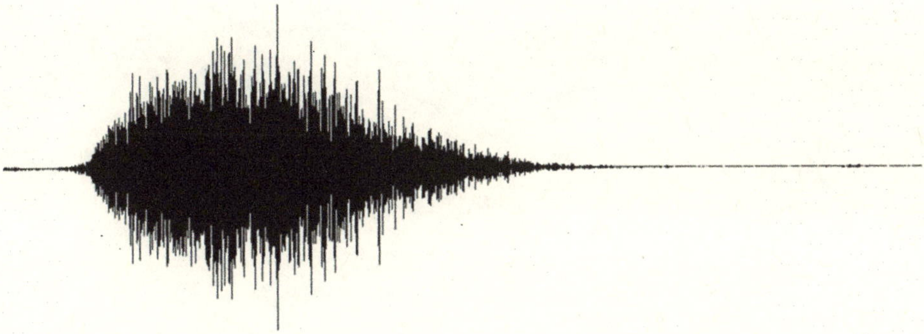

Fig. 2 – 00:02

Stigmata

In the episteme of grief many worlds will resemble a throat. I go down on a local prophet. As the spirit moves I'm carried along with his breath.

His few senses unspool. The pillowcase is a body bag for dreaming.

When we have clogged each other he shits on my fingers. I'm sorry, he tells me, that so much ruin is the accident of touch. I tremble there against his thigh, listening.

I return to the summer camp where I bury pastors in neat rows. Every night the guts of a sleeping bag cake to my chest.

In the morning I rehearse conversions over the picnic table's peeling skin. All my longing is entangled with defacement.

I recite an injunction in the woods. The killing gospel animates my speech.

A storm cloud curdles over his sleeping. I don't know what to do with the irrelation of things.

Without – between – he excretes – with again – again – a drip – he'll be mouthed – when near – in passing – a vacancy – among – within – he sputters – through – along his branch – out – along our belly – then again – who – in which world – his proboscis – which dialect – which slit – where – what debris – what flow – how often – when he's open – wherever he's open – only – a wake – only –

I gave up my most precious things: slouching, my bad knee, the comma. Our spacing will be a survival tactic though I will miss holding you in the shower and the films we never finished because we were horny.

The language of care retains its roots. A sickbed cut with lament. If care has a home it is the meeting place of grief and rest or the grief of a resting place or the resting place of grief. We attend to injury where we are injured. Care leaves us there. We're touching each other in its wreck.

II

Consecration to the Church Monster

this is my body in twelve shapes
this is my body in eleven shapes
this is my hung with suds fallen out
this is my razor burn
this is my blistered toe
this is my reckless towel

I found an altar with this inscription:
to the unknown god

I shrieked bright red and passed myself
to the clotted figure I sent wild
televangelisms as I beheld this lost rib

Noise V

here is a ruined sound
soft acoustic architecture
my household drone
when I broadcast
on the incontinent
frequency
this rending place
my shallow planet

Trouble Every Day, 2001

today on the sidewalk were
little mounds of stomach

I was sorry about the history of medicine
it was terrible for the film on my teeth

I was wrong about the little worm
the body was not a government

so much for the harmony of blood
now the part surrounds the whole

Noise VI

here the ruined sound
translates a common feeling
my sublingual gland
irrigates the sigh
here are the people
who clamour at the wreck
without them still
some language

The Garden, 1990

a pale pink condom in even
moisture buried for each loss

five pink pills swallowed in earth
only two decades later

pink carnations for stray isotopes
caught up in coming eddies

a rosy glow offset by violent clouds
contracting in its system wild pansies

where the quarantine breaks its frills
a deposit on long pink quiet

a very beautiful bearded iris has softened the decade

a very beautiful bearded iris is so bitterly hurt
in the wind it almost turns to dust in my hands

a very beautiful bearded iris is a great fuck

a very beautiful bearded iris that also has a right to live

a very beautiful bearded iris that might betray me

a very beautiful bearded iris has gone forward
an hour and died bruised by the salt spray

after three years' growth a beautiful bearded iris
that was once at the centre of a rose bed

Monday – the lilies have lasted eight days

Wednesday morning – all over the garden into the marsh
now years of gust that rattle in old blood

Wednesday afternoon – the accumulated front pages not
moving for many hours

Saturday – a full six weeks in advance of last year the
rosemary bushes are dying and the geraniums

the station's breath in a roar of steam
its cutting has grown into a little bush

a daffodil bulb with split skins leaking
oils on the mattress ablaze with mist and light

from an abundance – what a terrible god to take on the hurt
and hurt us all that day with no advice or medication

this land over which sweat passes like autumn rain

then in the hospice an acute exchange of thickets
the living bruise pooling there
a yield of flower the depletion of metre

owing to its breathing surface the sheets
that will not be stripped to residual emissions

beyond the soiled bed a memorial
to which no bloom subscribes

Monday – I pick deadheads off poppies and scatter the seeds

Wednesday – two days have passed in delirium feeling tangled

Tuesday morning – I have done this so many times before the fig has lost all its leaves

Monday – with so little time the events of the last year have left me

Saturday and Sunday – at the sea's edge he gathers him up in yesterday's foam

during this week I have explored my body on the bed of
imported leaves cascading or bushy overtaken by the haywire
clock on the wall the whole thing happens again where
during the long hours I watch the clock I wish it had gone
longer a descending hush with seeds

true scarlet is a problem
a crimson gash a ruby drop hanging
huge and scarlet the bright red berry a staunching
achillea a bloodwort and painful minutes
of hawthorn a donor of red camellia so tumescent
a bloody infection and the cottage sapped by pill a scarlet
runner sopping wet a gardening can of blood
burning dry in the drug's exhaust the aches
that plants will cure the roses are looking healthy
huge from last year and in flower

Secretion

only the spirit leaks
facing the waters only the spirit
confuses surface and depth only the spirit brings
its organs to me only the spirit distended

only the spirit is panoply of
breath and blood I cloud when speaking only
the spirit's malodour lake I wait
in the deluge for a first cause

Noise I

my plosive wound grinds meat
five-storey flame its mouth
now in power my animous wave
now in power my vulgate whelm
now in power my throat arithmetic
so that you break
heavy on me
here is a ruined sound

Fig. 3 – 00:03

Antichrist, 2009

there's no liturgy for today
the crepitus pine the trunk adorned
with holes the hurting ferns the fungus
gnat I don't want the grass
or the mulch that follows I tallied
the trees and became afraid

I've opened an account
now all flesh is strange and everyone agrees

as for what comes later the scriptures
are clear enough the awful heat of your breath
a foaming gap not the river I went dry
to the bridge and there was not even wind

Ninety-Five Theses on the Body

1. When we said intimacy we willed the entire life of the body to be one of confinement.

2. This word that cannot be understood as referring to the sacrament of being that is its emulsion.

3. But it does not mean touch. It can't touch you.

4. A spear breaks skin taps accumulated fluid in the membranes surrounding the lungs and drains an atrium. The smaller the love the greater the fear at once blood and water come out.

5. The blood and water contain our most private correspondences. I collect them in glass vials and circulate them through the storm drains on your block.

6. We neither desire nor are able to remit any bodies except those imposed by our own language. I worship ignorantly. I can't find you anywhere.

7. Are you hungry? When did you last eat?

8. We give ourselves thick each with the residue of the other.

9. When we give ourselves thick to the nonlocality of fucking so that we correlate only below the waist.

10. Blood is not life but the living subject as such. Blood is this endless unbroken unrest of welling forth.

11. In former times we imposed bodies not after but before gender as tests of contrition.

12. My rib my pituitary gland my ear.

13. In the city's urinary tract where I first became conscious of my continuities – the suspended bridge that resembles a spine.

14. This remnant smear that is to say my desire for imprecision.

15. Intimacy that didn't reduce to authenticity. Sound that didn't reduce to voice. Dysphoria that didn't reduce to body.

16. To say nothing of other things.

17. My rib my pituitary gland my ear seem to differ the same as this overpass this underpass this median.

18. Then there was a spill that disclosed the accident of embodiment.

19. Then there was a spill that widened our exposure.

20. Then there was a spill where skin washed away. Then there was a spill that washed you away.

21. I wish I had carried you. I carry you there. I carry you with me.

22. I wanted to nurture a lesion with you because I only understood disintegrated relation.

23. I wanted a blood under the body.

24. In its mouth in its mouth in its mouth.

25. Through which we couched in endless prepositions our approach to god.

26. Its blood under the body –

27. If we couldn't speak it – if we were left there –

28. If there had been no breath in common –

29. If we counted the forms – if you had been the gift –

30. If you had been innumerable –

31. Injury is done to the body when in the same poem more time is devoted to the self than to its guts.

32. I'm not sure whether all leaking souls wish to be saved.

33. I'm not sure of the malignancy of gender much less its remission.

34. No one lays hands with impunity on such fearsome abstractions as the existent and the nonexistent. Slowly upon touching them the blood congeals.

35. I'm sorry about the mess. I'm sorry about the symptoms of the mess.

36. I'm not sure he loves me like a hormone.

37. Every method opened to us. Every spirit appeared to us. Every scripture without lungs.

38. Was I sick with him?

39. As a child I watched my knuckles dry and crack through sermons then smeared them onto envelopes meant for tithes. I hid these envelopes only to return and note their shifts from deep red to brown.

40. Was I sick with him?

41. Once the skin on my rightmost knuckle buckled then split the meat broke open. The woman to my left covered her eyes the man to my right spit my blood from his mouth. My knuckle spray reached ten vertical feet. I twisted my hand the beam knocked a family from their pew.

42. It was the rhetoric of our gore. We were ideological in our filth.

43. Was I sick with you?

44. When I couldn't find your body I wrote a book to replace it. I wanted to mourn you while you were living.

45. I shall not eat anything with the blood.

46. I shall not make any cuttings in my flesh for the dead nor print any marks.

47. My gender was a stomach which is a mode of self-governance. It was hungry. It consumed all relation. Its digestion was an apology.

48. I puked for days. The carpet was an ocean. I know – never again will objects be solidly determined.

49. My rib my pituitary gland my ear.

50. I hold to curled anatomy. Sometimes there is a current of meat.

51. In its mouth in its mouth in its mouth.

52. So it will be as if I never loved you?

53. If we couldn't speak it – if it were elastic – if it were incontinent – if it were the glazed belly –

54. If it had no interior – if we had loved surface and after surface had we gone – if it were stretched –

55. If it were not a mouth.

56. If it were mouthed.

57. I have you recorded on my phone. I isolate scraps of your voice. I splice them into sentences that might retrieve or invent a memory. You can say anything. There can be your care. There can be your brutality. I can hold the fullness of our intimacy in the sound.

58. But there are too many of you. I didn't expect to be frightened.

59. Where you teach me weak theories of love.

60. Where you teach me transformation without justice. Where you teach me its aftermaths.

61. Where you teach me prayer as a practice of edging.

62. Where you teach me its mouthing. Where you teach me the salivary real.

63. Where you begin to resemble the thin film over my tongue. You thicken. You harden. You embed yourself in my soft palate. I study your presence there. I drool until our boundaries are translucent.

64. Already I'm inducing in myself a gender that is hairless and greedy for detachment.

65. This is a gloss on rage – a relentless assertion of my relation to you – it sounds like this – we go in spit – we go – beneath your tongue –

66. We go slipping – with – so we rage – we – muffled with longing –

67. I remember he was wearing a grey hoodie that was like most of his hoodies. I remember keeping very still and very quiet when he stopped moving so I could hear his breath. I remember I could smell his sweat.

68. Despite your best efforts I'm still slick with you.

69. Then we're bound to make bare nerve endings – we being raked – there is the liquid man – there is your appearance in deleted nudes –

70. There isn't any horizontality – there is the form being found – there is a hole –

71. Let him who speaks be anathema and accursed.

72. Let him who speaks be blessed and collapsed.

73. Where is the interplay of ducts. Where are the secretions. Where are the translations.

74. What is left uninterpreted in the economy of fluids is given over to god.

75. As if I have killed him – we say – even his hole –

76. On the contrary – we say it – we've been a skin on his surface – so we forgive you –

77. You're so hot. You're so reciprocal. You're so holy. You're so mucosal. You're so submissive. You're so nutritious. You're so cruel. You're so immiscible.

78. I will discharge it for you. I will emit it in sap for you.

79. In my final dream I love him again. We're in the city but geographical specificity works against me here so I won't explain further. If we have regrets we don't speak them. We don't speak at all. Language and location become accessory.

80. For that interval of rest. For that creeping sore of stain.

81. We will have to answer for you.

82. I want to go where the biological and historical are not consecutive. Where they are desire's most extreme collisions.

83. I want to go where a sphincter is not a mouth.

84. Where there are no teeth in the brain no striations in the meat no folds in the palms.

85. I've looked everywhere. I've consulted with every partition. Every rivulet. Every deep zipper. They don't know how to rebuild you. They all want a gentler topology.

86. I wanted to tender in you. I wanted to plant churches in you. I wanted to buy you a milkshake like the one I bought you after your first death. You couldn't drink it then. You wore two scarves. Your neck had been in flower.

87. Behold a rib. Behold an ear. Behold a pituitary gland. Behold a hunger to that gland.

88. I come quickly. I come to the city looking.

89. I've found your smallest and fastest intestine. I've found your survivorship bias. I've found your imprint in my unwashed sheets.

90. I'm sorry if I digested you. I didn't mean to digest you.

91. Away then with all those prophets who say peace peace peace and there is no peace.

92. Blessed be all those prophets who say cross cross cross and there is no cross.

93. In its mouth in its mouth in its mouth.

94. I want an unstained liver. I want a damaged finger. I want a loose and dreamy relation with my belly.

95. I want to go – where there is weeping for the body where there is mercy for the body where there are no names for the body.

Fig. 4 – 00:01

Notes

I wanted the "I" in these poems to be something stranger than a confessant. Not a speaker but a garburator. For some time I kept quiet, knowing that the imperative to speak would only bind me to the logic of a church, therapist, or market. At the same time, "I" wanted to speak, "I" needed to scream, "I" had to break up the quiet, even if I knew that my speech would be no less imposed than my silence. I began with the words of others. I didn't want to believe in property but couldn't shake my guilt. If not for guilt, would there be any difference between bibliography and confession?

"The Mystical Theology" draws from Pseudo-Dionysius's text of the same name, with a few detours into Teresa of Ávila's *The Interior Castle* and Francis of Assisi's biographies – namely, those by Bonaventure, Thomas of Celano, and Julian of Speyer. It also includes some language from Georges Bataille's *The Accursed Share* and *Inner Experience*, Maurice Blanchot's *The Writing of the Disaster*, Sigmund Freud's *The Interpretation of Dreams*, Sándor Ferenczi's "More About Homosexuality," and Jacques Derrida's *On the Name* and "Economimesis."

"Reparation" opens with a nod to Jean-François Lyotard's *The Differend*.

"The Garden, 1990" borrows its title from Derek Jarman's film *The Garden* and some of its text from diary entries collected in his *Modern Nature.*

"Ninety-Five Theses on the Body" shares text, structure, and half a name with Martin Luther's famous document, alongside a few lines from Luce Irigaray's *This Sex Which Is Not One*, Friedrich Nietzsche's *Philosophy in the Tragic Age of the Greeks*, G.W.F. Hegel's *Philosophy of Nature*, and the first volume of Michel Foucault's *History of Sexuality.*

Acknowledgments

Some of the poems collected here first appeared in *The Capilano Review*, *CV2*, *Glass Buffalo*, *Hart House Review*, *HELD*, and *PRISM international.* My thanks to the editors who welcomed and stewarded my work.

I can't thank Ryan Fitzpatrick and Catriona Strang enough for their warmth, patience, and guidance.

Thank you to Christine Stewart for tending to the earliest seeds of this collection.

I'm grateful for the poets, artists, and thinkers who have helped me to carry the weight of this little book. I can't hope to name you all, but a special thanks to iman adam, Alex Allen, Melody Chapin, James Collier, Merlin Cunniff, Tara M. Holman, Katherine E.A. Preston, and Z.Y. Yang.

Thank you to my brother and my parents, for your constancy, and to Nathan Maher Levy, for insoluble love.

Finally, thank you to Brittney Hubley and Mackenzie Wiebe – as poets, editors, and the best of friends.

Scott Jackshaw is a poet, scholar, and editor from Edmonton, Alberta. Their poetry and prose have appeared in journals including *The Capilano Review*, *CV2*, and *Jacket2*. They hold a PhD in English from Brown University.

Photo: Nathan Maher Levy